All I Can Gather & Give

Books by Patti Tana

How Odd This Ritual of Harmony (1981)

Ask the Dreamer Where Night Begins:
Poems & Postscripts (1986)

The River (1990)

Wetlands (1993)

When the Light Falls Short of the Dream (1998)

Make Your Way Across This Bridge:
New & Selected Writings (2003)

This Is Why You Flew Ten Thousand Miles (2006)

Any Given Day (2011)

Associate Editor of Poetry Anthology:
Raining Leaves (1986)
Edited by Maxwell Corydon Wheat, Jr.

Editor of Poetry Anthology:
Songs of Seasoned Women (2007)

All I Can Gather & Give

Poems by Patti Tana

Patti Tana

To Rosemarie

For your pleasure.

04/20/23

JB Stillwater Publishing
Albuquerque, New Mexico

Library of Congress Cataloging-in-Publication Data

Tana, Patti, 1945-
  [Poems. Selections]
  All I can gather & give : poems / by Patti Tana.
    pages cm
  ISBN 978-1-937240-45-5 (pbk.) -- ISBN 978-1-937240-46-2
(ebook)
  I. Title.

  PS3568.E615A6 2014
  811'.54--dc23

                              2014032616

        Acknowledgments on pages 87-89

20140915
JB Stillwater Publishing
12901 Bryce Avenue NE
Albuquerque, NM 87112
(505) 508-5513
jbstillwater.com

Printed in the United States of America

Dedication

to John, as always,
to our son Jesse,
to my beloved mother, Ada

Gratitude

Your responses helped me shape these poems:

Jesse Tana Renner, Gladys L. Henderson, Sharon Bourke, Mankh (Walter E. Harris III), Ruth Sabath Rosenthal, Adam Fisher, E. Willa Haas, Maxwell Corydon Wheat, Jr., Pramila Venkateswaran, Yolanda Coulaz, Les Schachter, Mary Gund, Elisa and Maryellen Raubach, and Elsbeth Renner for your encouraging conversations.

All I Can Gather & Give

You, you who spread your wings
studded with stars nightly
across the wide world,
> *what becomes of your glory?*

The many-limbed oak
framed by the hospital window
spreads wide to gather the sky,
> *scatters seeds over the earth.*

I lie here birthing & dying
in the serious business of blood,
my body open to
> *all I can gather & give.*

Contents

The Ally You Have Chosen

the naked man beside you
is the ally you have chosen
to walk with you through dreams
too real to awaken
and through life that is real as a dream

Desert Waterbed

what a long way we have come
from the waterbed in the desert

as we surveyed the scene from a flat roof
clouds would take shape in the distance
and move toward us with mounting power

everything was wet & dry
sun-drenched
bare & flourishing

Love Finds a Place

Love finds a place to live
some nearby park or patch of ground
yielding roots of an old tree
naked from years of rain and
touch even a doorway
the hard knob nudging you forward
into each other's arms

a stone bench provides a seat
a porch glider
a hammock
the private cocoon
of even the smallest car
can be comfortable
in Love's warm moist palm

anywhere there is space for two
there is space for one

first find Love
Love finds a place

Body Music

drawn together
in the barely-lit room
we give in to gray

dusk throws its cloak
over our bodies
one silhouette

inside my silk gown
your hand glides your bow
across my cello body

Yielding

pillow & mattress
receive the weight

the length & the breadth
of our bodies

welcome the pleasure
of lovers

Warm

not just at night
but in the afternoon
you come to me

warm above me
warm below me
warm within me

even my toes are warm

Rooted

hot, too hot
this August night
to wrap my body
'round your body
as you sleep
I twine my feet
with yours
and I am rooted

Field

you are the wind caressing my body
      I am the field

you are the rain filling my furrows
      I am the field

you plant the seeds that will flourish
      in the fields of time

Eros & Civilization

There he sat: Eros.
Here I sat: Civilization.

He wanted to seed;
I wanted to read.

After dialectical struggle
I decided to yield

my field to his plow.
When I satisfied

his need to breed,
I bred — he read.

Colorado Canvas

in a mountain pool newborn
cradled in our arms

rocky peaks & pine trees
spire to the sky

at night celestial light
streams through dark skies

landscape of memory
pool of my dreams

In This Dream

leaning back in a swing
       held by a vine-covered bough
              I watch the stream flow by

you hand me a string of purple
       beads that blossom
              into lilacs & lavender

filling my lap & spilling like laughter
                   into the stream

Reverie

unable to sleep
I travel to liquid realms
of reverie

Venetian canals
where stone angels dance
with shadows & light

Oahu's windward cliffs
lush green folds
draped in fog white

the Japanese bridge
in Giverny
where water lilies bloom

street lamps
haloed with morning mist
lead me home

We Stop to Watch

hurrying from thunder across the bridge
    we stop to watch
        bat wings flutter

lightning splits the sky
    spills across the pond

after the storm
    evening blesses the earth
        with a sky of burning roses

Sandy's Wake

strong winds thicken the air
    with the fury of leaves —
        skeletal branches become spears

we ride out the storm
    together in the dark
        dog between us quaking

morning reveals a hundred-foot tulip tree
    fallen across the garden
        sparing the red bridge and our home

you take your guitar in your arms
    and make the wood sing
        "Amazing Grace"

Kaleidoscope

the car glides smoothly
on the surface of the road
between mounds of splattered snow

the dog sticks her cinnamon-freckled face
between the front seats
you driving, me navigating

opening the window
I turn my face toward the sun
flickering through bare trees

closing my eyes I see
a dazzling kaleidoscope

Carousel

riding your equine body
        through moving circles of space
    my serpentine body
        becomes a wave of light

Charged

sleeping together
our bodies, charged particles,
align in the night

Soulstice

waking together
warm on solstice dawn
knowing days will grow

Pas de Deux

our bodies turn with the seasons

in each other's arms
we find shelter from winter storms

come spring we play tag all night
I touch you & you touch me

sweaty nights too hot to touch
we move in parallel

when autumn's chill draws us close
we feel again our skin on skin

Skin Knows Skin

The way the water spreads beneath the wind
      across the pond in widening waves
         of sparkling light —
the way a sleek, elegant animal arches
      into the palm of a familiar
        beloved hand —
   I tremble beneath your touch.

How can the body respond
      year after year
        to the same urges and delights?

Skin knows skin
      I say when you press into my body
        soft flesh and hard bones.
Skin loves skin
      your body replies
        stretched head to toe beside.

Ebb & Flow

I am the shore
your body washes

rivulet fingers
parting soft sand
flooding the land

my body ebbing
and flowing with yours

Love Should Be

simple
as slipping a ring on a finger
but is not.
It slips off
doing the dishes
is lost
diving from a cliff
or water-skiing on a desert lake
mislaid
on a nightstand in an unfamiliar room
on a second honeymoon
to celebrate your coming home.
When you circle back to find it
the circle is unbroken.

The forgetting

began as soon as I could remember, and yet
when I continue down the path, I come upon
what I forgot was stored in the brain
at the service of the mind, called up
by the mind's will to find what it seeks
in the brain's intricate warehouse.

We speak of memories "fading" and they are
washed out in time, diminished, obscured
by overload, need to be coaxed out of hiding
like a shy dog, the way my dog urges me
to walk with her, exercise, breathe deep,
keep those wheels oiled.

It's just that while everything is speeding up
I'm slowing down, and it takes time
to find the right word.

What a comfort to live in touch
with one who knows what I want to say
even when I remember
few
bare
words

Dear One

If I grow frail
gait unsteady,
will you wrap your arms around me
gently guide my step?

If dark seals my sight
and I lean
my head toward you,
will you stroke my hair?

If mind grants words
of just one beat,
will you hear my heart beat
dear one, dear one

Socrates Is a Man

Soothed by the rhythm of rain and the breath
of the man you love asleep beside you —
sirens invade your sleep and set you naked
on the wet slab of a city street
watching red lights race by.

The first lesson in logic taught in school
confirms what you already learned
the first time you saw the fish
floating at the top of the bowl:
Everything that lives — dies.
True for fish and true for men.

When he comes home with the results
you say take the test again.
Embracing you, he offers philosophically,
"We're all going to die of something.
I've had a great life."

That night when sirens pierce your sleep
you push away the image of shivering
on the street, red lights racing by,
and wrap your body around him.

If You Leave

Leave your coat on the back of the chair
      by the door.

Leave your keys in the bowl
      your shoes on the floor near the bed.

I will keep everything you touched
      exactly where it is —

everything that holds your touch.

Into the Unknown

If I should go before you
      silence heavy in our home

let your grief be light
      let your joys be long.

Imperfect Circles

I am resolved to live with imperfection.

You put your whole self in —
that's what it's all about.

Appointment

Shutting windows to September chill
I watch a bee skim the surface of the glass.
Since the swarm of yellowjackets stung me
as I walked by a clump of white feather hosta
and landed in the hospital,
I don't see flowers the same way.
Now I see the sting in the bloom.

Again this month we mourn
the loss of so many lives
whose death was delivered by a plane.
Now I know that mine could be delivered
by a vessel no bigger than a peanut.

"Forewarned is forearmed"
Mama would say, so I promise her picture
I will not go barefoot in the inviting grass
I will wear long sleeves and carry an Epipen,
though I know some day I will die
            even if I flee all the way to Samarra.

The Executioner Wore Gloves

After she locked the dog in the house
she put on her gloves and reached for the spray.
Hornets had built a nest on the garage
where she and the dog had to walk.

Sure, she told herself, she was doing it
to protect herself and the dog
who'd jump at anything that moved,
bite a bee out of the air & swallow it.
Still, she had no taste for killing,
would have left them alone
if they weren't a threat.

No breeze seemed to stir
but the poison blew back in her face.
Though she tried to hold her breath
till she ran in the house, death
clings to her gloves, her throat, her lungs,
keeps coming up in her spit
as she writes this apology.

Of Boys and Men

Home from camp all flushed and angry
the son says he tried to stop
boys from torturing frogs, begged
his counselor to make them stop
but the man said, "Boys will be boys."

His father tells him a childhood story
about stopping kids from throwing stones
at a cat tied to a post.
They talk about the pain
of cats and frogs and boys.

When they take a walk after dinner
they're careful to step over worms
that surfaced after rain.

Scars

In the summers of our childhood, my mother
took me and my brothers to Bear Mountain
to see bears in a zoo across a high walkway.

I was afraid of falling from high places
so my big brother would scare me by leaning
way over the railing and pretending to slip.

On a lake named for dead Hessians, he'd fish
with worms wiggling on a hook, yank the hook
from the bloody mouth, and toss back the fish.

There was an archery range he liked so much
Mom bought a bow and arrows that he'd shoot
in our yard at a large target stuffed with straw.

I was the tag-along little sister fetching arrows.
I don't know what I said, but he warned me,
"If you open your mouth again, I'll shoot you."

When I silently opened my mouth, he shot me
in the left knee. The tip of the arrow was blunt
so it didn't pierce the bone, but there was blood

and I still wear the scar.

True Stories

All this talk
about what goes on
in locker rooms and pews
behind closed classroom doors
the steel cage of a car
on a deserted road
hand on your knee
in a dirty basement
buried too deep
for people who don't want to hear
your scream

conjures up the shadow
of my big brother
flashlight in hand
pulling down my covers
and me jumping up
to push him down the stairs.

Elephants in Chains

Like elephants in chains
who pull themselves free
to race for higher ground
when the earth trembles

you must free yourself.

Hidden Poems

How far is the country of longing?
How close the nearest pain?
Let the poem be your map.

And what about the poems you hide
even from yourself?

You know, the ones you crumple in small fists
and stuff in pockets
or tear up and bury in the bottom of the trash

until they rise again
demanding you give them shape.

Write them on your skin.
See how the body bears your scars.

Tattoo

the constellation of dark stars
reminds me
of my origin & destination

long after I stepped
down from the hospital table
with four dark marks
circling my breast
to target the searing beam

Likewise

Striding across a field of wild flowers
the confidence of innocence
nakedness concealed.

Likewise striding toward her
blossom in her hair
the confidence of experience
nakedness revealed.

Eve Offered

When she touched
the soft curves of her breasts
hard curves of her hips
the cheeks of her buttocks

when she offered
her thighs as a cushion
to lead him inside
the crimson chamber

the naked man
entered paradise.

Appetites

Using a new knife
I did not know its power.
What appetites it unleashed!

Someone Brings a Loaf of Bread

What to do with the bread, he wonders,
trying to resist temptation. He'd throw it out
but knows it's rude to refuse a gift.

Slicing through the hard crust, he reveals
the soft center, brushes it with olive oil, dots it
with fresh garlic, wraps it in foil for the oven.

Warm smells radiating from the kitchen
fill his body even before the long, savory boats
sail to the table.

And look! There sits the basket of bread, ample
center of the circle, host and guest
joined in the breaking of bread.

The Remains

Early morning trucks
rumbling through my sleep
stop to collect the remains
of indulgences hastily gobbled.

I wake to thank the priests
who take away.

Romping with the Spirits

at night the spirits
of the living & the dead
rise from their bodies
in the ground & the bed
to dance in the air
dance in the air

last night the shade of a youth
stole into my room as I slept
& we romped like puppies
into the dawn

when I asked
where did you go?
he laughingly waved
his arms in the air & was gone

Awkward Hearts

Too shy to sign my name to the valentine
I made for the first boy I ever loved,
hurriedly I wrote *G-u-s-s W-h-o*
and stuffed it in the gaudy box
in Miss Brook's fourth grade class.

There it waited with the other cards
until a classmate gave them out,
my eyes darting to see his smile
when he opened mine, but instead
I heard a hearty laugh: "Guss Who?
G-U-S-S Who? Who's 'GUSS'?"

How old could I have been? Nine?
Though more than fifty years have passed
I can feel the heat rise up my neck
to color my face as red as the thick
construction paper we used
to cut those awkward hearts.

I never told him it was me
who left the "e" out of "Guess,"
I just kept writing love poems
and on every one I signed my name.

Bashert

It's been years since I've heard him humming,
since I heard the giggle in his voice
as he spoke on the phone
with one who could have been
his *bashert.*

Whatever it is now that makes you smile
at some shared mystery,
may the fleeting joy that lights your face
stay with you. And when you catch a glimpse
of yourself in the glass beaming back
may it feel right.

Retired

In 1903, the first box of Crayola crayons
contained 8 colors and cost 5 cents:
red, orange, yellow, green, blue,
brown, violet, black.
The box grew to 64 colors by 1958
and included a sharpener,
till 1990 when the company "retired" 8 colors:
lemon yellow, orange yellow, orange red,
violet blue, green blue, blue gray,
raw umber, and even the lovely maize.

In the 1982 film "Blade Runner," set in 2019,
the authorities "retired" renegade replicants
(meaning they "destroyed" them)
after the almost-human robots they created
had served 4 years of slavery.

My dog sleeps when she's tired,
wakes when she's rested,
eats when she's hungry,
plays when she's bored,
snuggles when she wants to be stroked.

That's retired.

The Widow

makes a list
      every morning

checks it off
      throughout the day

goes to bed
      after dinner

dreams all night
      in his arms

Down to the Bone

Mama used a bar of soap
down to the bone,
rubbed the crackled stub
between her palms
until it disappeared.
"Waste not, want not."

She said it's a sin to throw out food
while people go hungry,
tucked her empty perfume bottles
into drawers uncapped
to catch the last bouquet.

When she died at ninety-seven
nothing was wasted
nothing thrown away.
I hold every ounce of life
she poured into my soul.

Sometimes when I visit her
room, I spray *White Shoulders*
in the air
to breathe in her scent.

Sheik's & Barney's

To put food on the table, my mother worked
as a waitress at *Sheik's & Barney's*
after her department store job. She'd leave
the house in her spotless white uniform,
hankie she embroidered with bright thread
blooming from her breast pocket,
and a big apron to hold notepad, pen, and tips.

Her boss told her he valued her service, but didn't
even pay her minimum wage
so the tips were most of her earnings.
In the morning she'd spill the coins
from her apron onto the kitchen table
and I'd help sort and stack and roll them
into paper tubes of different colors
to exchange for bills at the bank.

Silver dollars she saved in a black purse
in her closet "for emergencies," so we never
felt broke. In fact, my brothers and I felt blessed
every night when my mother called from work
to give us the blessing her father had given her.

One morning as we counted at the kitchen table
she told me that after she served more bread, more
wine, after she cleared the dishes, a man waved
some cash at her yelling, "Come here, Sweetheart!"
When she reached out her hand, he tore up
the bills and dropped them on the floor.

In the silence that followed, blood rose
up her neck and flushed her cheeks.
It was the first time she'd felt this particular
humiliation, so it was hard to swallow
her words, but being a lady
she turned and walked to the kitchen.

I'd like to say that Barney barreled
through the swinging doors, that he told
the bastard off, that he made good
on the money still on the floor,
but I don't remember that.

What stays with me is her dignity.
In spite of sore feet and back, she didn't
dump a pitcher of ice water in that man's lap.
My mother turned and walked into the kitchen
so she could put food on our table.

The Blessing

When a young woman took shelter in my home
I tucked her in to sleep with the blessing
Papa gave to my mother
and she passed on to me:
Good night, good luck, God bless you,
pleasant dreams, I love you, and zi-ga-zint,
stroking her hair with each phrase
the way my mother did.
The woman wept:
"No one ever blessed me."

In the morning, we packed her clothes
in sturdy bags and drove to the station
where she asked me to bless her again.
She wondered how her life might have been
if someone had blessed her, and that
made me think of the blessings I gave her,
my hands on her head, as a kind of shelter,
an invisible shawl she would take with her.

Harmonica

Late at night the house breathes
what sounds like harmonica chords
drifting across the prairie
to a wide river rolling through the night.

In her last months
my mother would hear a choir
singing songs that she sang as a girl
and we'd sing along.

O Shenandoah, I love your daughter
A-way, you rolling river
For her I'd cross your roaming waters
A-way, I'm bound to go, 'cross the wide Missouri.

My Mother's Gifts

My mother heard the angels sing
before she died,
before the smile that sealed her lips
stilled her voice.

Now I hear her in the soothing
sound of water tumbling over stones
outside my window, and in the leaves
the wind makes tremble.

Among the gifts my mother gave to me
is this treasure: my mother heard the angels
sing before she died
and now I hear her song.

Posture

Even in death, my mother
has good posture.

Sitting in a straight-backed chair
pushing against the pain
her eyes look forward
not down.

She walks across the room
shoulders balanced as a beam
wings guiding her toward me.

Wild Roses

When I see roses growing wild
branches jutting every which way
spilling over the garden wall
blossoms open wide to show their gold
in a burst of wild beauty,
I hear my mother calling me "Maggie,"
her wild child, laughing as she chased me
'round the table with a brush
to tame my tangled hair.

Imperfect Circles

In the pool at the Y, babies splash
in mothers' arms, as mine did years ago,
forming an irregular circle.

Shaky the Shark and Baby Shark
Mama Dolphin and Baby Dolphin
rolling in the waves.

The mothers sing *You put your right hand in,*
your right hand out, right hand in
and you shake it all about.

Laughter pours from the babies
as they whirl in weightless flight
when mothers sing *you turn yourself around*

Everything dissolves in water —
the spot, the scar, the sag.
I am resolved to live with imperfection.

The locker room hair dryer is broken.
So what if the circle is not perfectly round?
You put your whole self in —
   that's what it's all about.

Every Season Has Its Beauty

Seeing our bodies age
I think of trees
in their bare beauty.

Berth

Some yearn for the graveyard in the sky.
        Others settle in water, fire, earth.

Give my soul a welcome berth
        in the body of this life, so I can keep
                tacking in the winds of paradise

The Summer Volunteer

climbs out the window box and in the window
tendrils coiling everything it touches
heart-shaped leaves sprouting from thick vines.

Yellow blossoms pucker in the joints
where leaf-stalk joins the stem
becoming bulbous amber gourds in fall.

No one planted magic beans.
The vine took root between geraniums
and sucked the sun until it sang

Store up sunshine —
Soon the cold will close the window
Soon the wind blows leaves away
Lift O lift your face and store the sun!

Heat Wave

I ride out the wave
sitting still on the porch
fanned by the quivering leaves

After Rain

gray gives way to blue
and the green-brown peaty scent
of wet grass and soil

earthworms everywhere
one loud cricket
many gulping frogs

Weathering

I, too,
catch the leaves
racing furiously in autumn's wind —

Dried leaves
weather in the vase
where it's always autumn.

Every Season Has Its Beauty

Walking the woods after rain
    when I touch saplings
        they shower me.

Caught in the branches
    the moon blooms clearer
        as leaves fall.

Seeing our bodies age
    I think of trees
        in their bare beauty.

First Frost

The window frames a full moon
    hanging like a lantern
        in bare trees.

Within this house, safe
    from the whip of winter,
        the dog nudges the covers with her nose.

When I let her in
    I sleep like a stone
        skipping across a moonlit sea.

Husbandry

Careful not to break snow-laden branches
weighted till they almost touch the earth,
he brushes off their burden.

Snow Legs

These winter storms
chase each other up the coast
before snow has a chance to melt.

Wading through snow thigh high
dog leaping like a doe before me
I feel again my childhood confidence.

If I fall, soft white cold would cushion me,
swallow me. I could lie here
safe within the belly of the whale
        as it carries me up the coast to Maine

Earth Is Rich

Dull brown comes alive
in woods where earth is rich
with years of leaves becoming soil
with bark, with feathers,
and the moist brown pile
dogs leave steaming in the morning air.

Maggie's Coat

How we longed for warmth this winter.
Ice kept us shut inside.
Only the dog's insistent needs
forced us out to brave the cold.

Suddenly the temperature rose
just a tease, then a few days later
we didn't have to brace against the raw.

As Maggie runs through the woods
stopping to nose the earth beneath the snow
her patchwork coat of brown & white
looks like autumn leaves through snow.

And when she comes inside the house
she wears the map of winter's thaw.

The Stepping-on-the-Coat Ceremony

couldn't have started in Ohio.
I never wanted that winter to end.
First winter away from home
I found love beneath the lamppost
in front of Humanities Hall,
snow gently covering my hair as we kissed
in the night & in the morning
the Dean's warning
about Public Displays of Affection.

We must have started making a ceremony after
we moved back East where sometimes
seasons get stuck. Like this one.
Well past April Fool's, I thought
we were through with the second blanket
when in blows a raw gust of wind
and nasty precipitation.

This year we'll have to wait till May
to carry our coat up a hill in the sun,
to step on the coat & declare with a flourish
winter is finished!

Elation

when you are happy
my heart

light on the wings of spring

sails in the currents
of eternal now

You Know It's Spring

when the red
truck

and the white
shed

showing through bare
trees

are curtained by green

Easter Morning

for Lillianna

When I found a carrot on the roof of my car
earth still clinging to the tip of the root
I ate it — greens, sweet root, earth & all.

Glad

Rocking on the porch
in early April warm

glad the bugs are back.

Buddha's Smile

Morning quiet
draws me to the garden
wet with dew.

Suddenly a robin
sings *cheerily*
on Buddha's head.

First Came the Egg

nestled on the isthmus between two ponds.
A pair of geese floating nearby
watch the pointer who's sniffing around
till I call her away.

Then came the fox, smaller than the dog
— a flame of autumn in spring —
making its way up the rise
on the far side of the big pond
nosing every twig in the woods.

I sit on a bench with the dog
between fox and egg
wondering what I can do to protect them.
When the dog runs toward the woods
I call her back.

Brooding

Reed by reed, a pair of swans built a nest
on the shore of the pond behind our house
and then she sat, and sat, for well over a month.
She'd stretch out her neck to eat what floated by
while her mate patrolled the pond for invaders.
As she grew thinner, she'd leave the nest
to flap her soiled wings in the pond.
At night he'd rest near her in the water.

Finally on a Sunday morning, one, then two,
then three tiny fuzzy cygnets popped up
from beneath her body
and soon there was another.
Father led them into the water
while mother stayed on the nest, waiting.
Later that day, a fifth one emerged to complete
the yearly brood: two white and three gray.

Well, we said, all that time on the nest
was worth it, and kept camera & binoculars handy.
Through a week of hard rain, the family stayed
together in the nest or on the pond,
cygnets clustered close behind the mother
or carried on her back, or strung out in a line,
father keeping watch at the end of the parade.
And then the countdown began.

One by one they disappeared overnight
clenched in the jaws of a giant snapping turtle,
muskrat or raccoon, perhaps a fox.
We didn't know.
The count would hold steady for a few days
then in just the turn of a head
another would be gone,
the last one right before our eyes:

Sunset calls us to the porch, blue clouds streaking
a pink sky reflected in the water. Suddenly a hawk
tears open the sky with the last cygnet clutched
in its talons. Wings slapping wildly on the surface
of the pond, the big swan rushes after them
till he hits shore.
Young one gone, he drifts toward his mate —
long neck a flat line on the water.

Morning finds them next to each other in the nest.

Circling

the *whoosh* of wings
draws my eyes skyward

two swans flying figure eights
around my neighbor's home & mine

in a seamless sign
of infinity

Absence of Pain

Not in prelude to prayer
more clumsy than humble
you fall on your knees
when you trip on a root
while walking your dog
and the dog licks your face
as you stare at the ground
pain shooting from knees
up your thighs to your back
where it simmers for days
till you make a small turn
and a flash of raw pain
stops the flow of your day
a red thread of pain
laces your life
reminding you that
the absence of pain
can't be taken for granted.

When I Come Home from the Hospital

peonies have spent their extravagant glory
but the roses (O the roses!) are blazing
& honeysuckle offers its sweet neck to taste
as I walk with the dog through the trails
in the woods & the woods are calling
Welcome home! Welcome home!

Index

Acknowledgments

My thanks to the editors of publications in which these poems first appeared:

String Poet, Ed. Annabelle Moseley: "Snow Legs," "Harmonica" (stringpoet.com)

Cyclamens and Swords, Ed. Johnmichael Simon and Helen Bar-Lev: "Romping with the Spirits," "The Summer Volunteer," "The forgetting," "Posture," "The Blessing," "Every Season Has Its Beauty," "Rooted," "Awkward Hearts," "Retired," "All I Can Gather & Give" as "What Becomes" (cyclamensandswords.com)

Long Island PULSE Magazine, Ed. Nada Marjanovich: "Body Music" as "Dusk," "Wild Roses" (lipulse.com)

Voices Israel 2011, Ed. Johnmichael Simon: "Maggie's Coat," "Kaleidoscope"; *Voices Israel 2012*: "Socrates Is a Man," "Down to the Bone"; *Voices Israel 2013*: "Love Should Be," "Body Music"; *Voices Israel 2014*: "Bashert," "Hidden Poems"

Paws, Claws, Wings and Things (2012), Ed. James P. Wagner (Ishwa) and Nick Hale: "Kaleidoscope," "Maggie's Coat"

Whispers and Shouts (2012), Ed. Gail Goldstein and Judy J. R. Turek: "Scars," "The Remains"

CCAR Journal, 2012: "Dear One"; *CCAR Journal 2013*: "Elephants in Chains." Copyright 2012 and 2013 by Central Conference of American Rabbis. Used by permission of Central Conference of American Rabbis. All Rights Reserved.

PPA Literary Review, 2012, Ed. Cliff Bleidner: "Buddha's Smile"; *PPA Literary Review, 2013*: "Wild Roses"; *PPA Literary Review, 2014:* "Hidden Poems"

2013 HAIKU CALENDAR, Ed. Mankh (Walter E. Harris III): "Glad," "within this house, safe / from the whip of winter" from "First Frost"; *2014 HAIKU CALENDAR:* "Heat Wave," "You Know It's Spring"

Soul-Lit: a journal of spiritual poetry, Ed. Wayne-Daniel Berard: "Absence of Pain"

Think Long Island First, Ed. Ewa Rumprecht: "Sandy's Wake" (thinklongisandfirst.com)

Soul Fountain, Ed. Tone Bellizzi: "Soulstice," "Berth," "Circling," "My Mother's Gifts" as "Gifts"

Perfume River Poetry Review, Ed. Vuong Quoc Vu: "Eve Offered" (touranepoetrypress.wordpress.com)

Jewish Women's Literary Annual (2014), Ed. Henny Wenkart and Sheri Lindner: "Imperfect Circles," "Sheik's & Barney's"

Literature Today, Ed. Dr. Pradeep Chaswal and Dr. Deepak Chaswal: "First Came the Egg"

Changing Harm to Harmony: Bullies and Bystanders (2014), Ed. Joe Zaccardi: "Of Boys and Men"

First Literary Review-East, Ed. Cindy Hochman and Karen Neuberg: "Yielding" (rulrul.4mg.com)

The Nassau Review, Ed. Christina M. Rau: "Brooding"

The Whirlwind Review, Ed. Jill Jepson: "The Executioner Wore Gloves" (writingthewhirlwind.net)

The following poems were published in previous books of poems by Patti Tana:

"Eros & Civilization" and "Love Finds a Place" in **How Odd This Ritual of Harmony** (Gusto Press, 1981) and **Make Your Way Across This Bridge: New & Selected Writings** (Whittier Publications, Inc., 2003)

"Skin Knows Skin" in **This Is Why You Flew Ten Thousand Miles** (Whittier Publications, Inc., 2006)

"The Ally You Have Chosen" is the last stanza of "The Naked Man," in **This Is Why You Flew Ten Thousand Miles** (Whittier Publications, Inc., 2006) and **Any Given Day** (Whittier Publications, Inc., 2011).

The following poems received an award:

"Eros & Civilization," C. W. Post Poetry Center 1979, Jeanne Welcher, Director

"Every Season Has Its Beauty" (last stanza), Performance Poets Association 2013, Cliff Bleidner, Coordinator

"Imperfect Circles," Mid-Island Y Poetry Series 2014, Gayl Teller, Director

"Hidden Poems," Performance Poets Association 2014, Cliff Bleidner, Coordinator

About the Author

Patti Tana grew up in the Hudson River Valley, and she has made her home on Long Island. She is Professor Emerita of English at Nassau Community College (SUNY), where she received The Faculty Distinguished Achievement Award. From 1999 to 2003, she was the Coordinator of the Creative Writing Project. The Walt Whitman Birthplace Association selected her as their 2009 Long Island Poet of the Year.

Her poems have been published in the *Anthology of Magazine Verse & Yearbook of American Poetry*, and they have been awarded first prize from the Shelley Society of New York, Long Island Poetry Collective, Lake Ronkonkoma Historical Society, Performance Poets Association, *The Nassau Review*, Peninsula Public Library, and *Xanadu: A Literary Journal*.

The poet was Artist-in-Residence at the Volcano Arts Center on the Big Island of Hawaii in 1989. Since it was founded in 1990, she has been associate editor of the *Long Island Quarterly*. She is associate editor of the poetry anthology *Raining Leaves* (1986) and editor of *Songs of Seasoned Women* (2007). *All I Can Gather & Give* is Patti Tana's ninth collection of poems.

Visit *pattitana.com* to listen to Patti read her poems.

Other Titles from

JB Stillwater Publishing Company

A Thousand Doors
Matt Pasca
ISBN: 978-0-9845681-6-1
Binding: Paperback and eBook

Pasca's work pays homage to Kisa Gotami's quest to save her son by finding a home where, impossibly, no suffering has befallen the inhabitants. In the end, *A Thousand Doors* testifies to the necessity of sharing our stories with courage and vulnerability, and how doing so can lead us further down the path of joy.

Over Exposed: A Poetic Memoir
Terri Muuss
ISBN: 978-1-937240-23-3
Binding: Paperback and eBook

In the pages that follow, Muuss brings us close to what we might describe as the secret war, the intimate war, which resides in closed rooms, in seemingly ordinary homes. Yet these poems are written, reader, with such delicacy, such concern for image, for pause, and purpose-for, in fact, beauty. Yes, these poems and prose pieces turn on the beauty of poetry, of what art can accomplish. I bid you open the book. It is a miracle. -- Veronica Golos

Something Like Life
Barbara Novack
ISBN: 978-1-937240-09-7
Binding: Paperback and eBook

In this neat and intelligent book of poetry *Something Like Life* author Barbara Novack describes the often subliminal messages that are sent to us every day in the beauty and sadness we often see around us in nature and human experience. This book is poetry at its best.

Serenity and Beauty
Rita Mosiman
ISBN: 978-1-937240-19-6
Binding: Paperback and eBook

As an avid hiker feeling a strong connection to the land and nature's artistry, I decided to create an art book, which will hopefully assuage the gloomy clouds of recent global economic woes. Nature is inspiring, soothing, exciting, and powerful. It helps us to remember that true beauty in life exists in the simplest of things, which reach every soul open to them if only we look, sense, and feel.

Orphan Thorns
Lynn Strongin
ISBN: 978-1-937240-06-6
Bindings: Paperback and eBook

In this touching and often heart wrenching book, Lynn Strongin explores the beauty of the human soul and its ability to rise above physical as well as psychological illness.

Orphan Thorns: A Brush with Genius
Lynn Strongin
ISBN: 978-0-9845681-4-7
Bindings: Paperback and eBook

In this collection of late works by Lynn Strongin, we find that perfect balance of salt and water spiced with symbolism and metaphor that poet Strongin does so well. Jewish Temple offerings included salt and Jewish people still dip their bread in salt on the Sabbath as a remembrance of those sacrifices.

NOTES

Made in the USA
Charleston, SC
03 October 2014